Just the Basics By Emolyne

Ruth E. Molyne

This edition of "Just the Basics by Emolyne" is made possible by the generous support of a grant from the Virginia Region IV Partnership of Community Service Boards.

Bloomington, IN

authorHOUSE®

Milton Keynes, UK

AuthorHouse™
1663 Liberty Drive, Suite 200
Bloomington, IN 47403
www.authorhouse.com
Phone: 1-800-839-8640

AuthorHouse™ UK Ltd.
500 Avebury Boulevard
Central Milton Keynes, MK9 2BE
www.authorhouse.co.uk
Phone: 08001974150

First published by AuthorHouse 1/29/2007

ISBN: 978-1-4259-8821-0 (sc)

Library of Congress Control Number: 2006911178

Printed in the United States of America
Bloomington, Indiana

This book is printed on acid-free paper.
The Holy Bible, New American Standard (NASB), B.B. KIRKBRIDE

Bible Co., Inc, Indianapolis, IN, 1983

Contents

Preface

Just the Basics *(JTB)* is a very simple technique of introspection, development of increased self love (or self knowledge) and appreciation, and behavior modification via consistently redefining knowledge and having great expectations of good things transpiring in one's own life. **JTB** is a dynamic of character building. Segments of passages from the Holy Bible, I Timothy 4:16, suggests that you pay close attention to yourself and your own teaching and to persevere in these things. *JTB* is designed to help you create a more positive mirror image in order to hear yourself think and speak as you should for the purpose of tearing down mental strongholds that hamper spiritual, emotional, physical, and financial growth and development. The modus operandi of *JTB* will help you, the student of life, learn to overcome challenges ranging from the sublime to the ridiculous, thereby arriving at true happiness which emanates from within.

Acknowledgements

I would like to thank Chanda Bass for her friendship and kindness in proof reading drafts and for the input she has so graciously provided. Special thanks goes to the myriad spiritual advisors for their willingness to share God's word and so much more their examples of applied wisdom bringing about that inspiration to pass on to others what has been shared with me. For my figle (that's Italian for children) Minika Janée, an attitude of gratitude for her talents in reading and suggestions regarding the manuscript, and Carla Ginyne for her inspirational love of life, and the eyes of their enlightenment, John and Claude and bunches of hugs for their unspoken faith that God would work miracles in our lives. To my nepoti (that's Italian for grandchildren) Michael Jawon, Jayla Wyethia, and Skylar Nadir as their glorious lights shine brightly reminding the world that the wholeness of their own spirit prevails and so greater works are still to be done. To my brother Kevin Miles and my mother Minnie Belle for their dedicated work in accomplishing God's plan for their lives, to my father, James Baker (aka Cutter), and his family for their love of life and to the myriad extended family and friends, thanks for being the great individuals that you are!

Introduction

The purpose of **Just The Basics** (JTB) is to help all people to see themselves more clearly as the positive, forward thinking, and successful winners that they are. This is accomplished via mind expansion which is simply another way of saying that you are willing to consistently redefine at a more qualitative intellectual level, your understanding of life. Mind expansion is the process of developing the courage to share your new understandings with others. Intense introspection is a necessity in mind expansion because it helps in maintaining mental stamina, dream building and goal setting, milestone planning, implementation of mid course corrections, and in due time the experience of more purposeful living. Another component of the JTB school of thought is faith, or having the ability to believe that you are worthy of the many blessings that you see yourself as having the potential to obtain, even before it looks anything like your ideas are going to come true.

Throughout the book I will use symbolism, analogies, and elementary grammatical ideas to show how the intelligence that you already possess can be modified behaviorally to maintain level paths for your feet and enhance clarity in your mind to bring about the fulfillment of your dreams and goals.

Focus Focus Focus

Just The Basics By Emolyne **(JTB)** is a life re-covery model designed to help you understand that you have all that is required to obtain your highest dreams and goals and to help you to become <u>intro-spective at all times</u>. This means understanding in all situations, what a particular circumstance "means to you". When I was a little girl playing in the projects of 21st Street in Newport News, VA, the kids would walk around saying "what it mean to me?" Little did I know that I was actually quoting something that was probably being passed through the air as a "stop and think" note, which is a requirement for having a conscious healthy spiritual walk in life.

It is written, that once an established goal is accomplished, you must have a large dream in sight, because the energy required to accomplish turning the former dream into a goal and bringing it to light will have to be complemented with the consistent expectation of completion of further endeavors. Otherwise, the now loose energy that was harnessed in the form of a catalyst for the former dream could become a depressant, and transform into mediocre, rather than goal directed thinking. It is also written that an individual's thought processes can improve or destroy their ability to reach taller planes of intellectual consciousness. Therefore it is important to be working towards the manifestation of a greater dream, that is, having your vision in the forefront of your mind at all times, especially when reaching out to others. You will have to be careful though, that your relationships are developed in the light of how you can impart experience, wisdom, resources, etc., for the purpose of helping others to excel, because when you help others you will naturally be helping yourself.

Reference to your dream and persistent introspection are fundamental. Society has rightfully imparted the idea that sharing of one's own knowledge is imperative if spiritual growth and development, financial freedom, and global harmony are to be experienced. Some say that you can't keep wisdom unless you give it away. When you take the time to communicate how you think, to others, it helps to produce more meaningful relationships. The Holy Bible passage of Matthew 28:19 states to "go therefore into all the world and make disciples of all the nations....". I believe that you can also see that statement as "go into the world and decipher all your words to the nations" (people). Life is a symbolic experience, therefore the human being is considered the nation. One of the features of the **JTB** model is to sound words and phrases to yourself so that the thought can be modified for the purpose of mentally clearing your pathway as you spiritually walk through life to continue on in progress. The procedure of **_using your own ideas_** or **_conscious thinking_** is considered to be an **_"up"_** or **_upstairs_** level. And the conscious application of your intelligence is what living <u>on earth</u> is about. Sometimes life is like an airport with numerous airplanes in the air trying to land but a severe thunderstorm may appear to be keeping the progression in abeyance. **JTB** will help you to stay above the circumstances and maintain harmony and clarity of mind as you move beyond, above, or through whatever life has decided to deposit along your path as a test to determine whether you are saying what you mean and meaning what you say. In the past, biblical writings have called it letting "your ya be your ya". Please note that without the practice of introspection, the sharing of one's gifts may become inappropriate giving that distracts the provider from their own dreams/goals resulting in unhappiness, and the belief that life is void because it may seem that they are giving without any consciousness of return. However, a person has to come to recognize that the example established by their living and application of their wisdom is the most important thing that can be given to others. When self appreciation is erased by extensive living outside of self, the giving becomes a weapon, and control issues concerning other people arise.

One of my favorite motivational speakers, Birdie Yager, says: "the secret to living is giving", and I concur. You can truly only realize your dreams if you are helping others to see the manifestation of their dreams. It is good to note on the other hand, that in the process of giving there is the risk of losing yourself and forgetting your purpose for being on planet earth, which is simple and vital to remember, "I exist to help the world to become a better place in which to live by being the best person that I can be".

If you did not need to remember your own dreams and aspirations in the midst of it all, then all humans would probably have green eyes and be the same complexion and have identical thoughts at all times.

I think Adolph Hitler was prejudiced to this degree and I recall a physician who was successful at applying the Alcoholics Anonymous (AA) principles to his life stating that, "Hitler was a classic example of an alcoholic who did not drink and did not go to AA meetings". Apparently he chose to try and change the core of other people, rather than himself. Some aspects of **JTB** will reflect that change is pretty much the only constant in life, hence now the AA acronym can also be symbolic of _A_ttitude _A_djustment. I sense that the gist of Hitler's madness was that a great number of people were not to his liking. He must have forgotten that each person is created in their own likeness, that of God him/herself. The dislike and envy of others is a mind-set that is frequently encountered when individuals pay too little attention to themselves, or the insides become turned outward with proper direction being lost, if you will. When the mind is operating like that you may develop amnesia concerning what your own dreams and goals are. And you can also become instrumental in obstructing the pathways of others when they begin to stand up for what they believe in and remove themselves as your easy access comfort zone in order to accomplish greatness in their own lives. That kind of stronghold is a very inconspicuous form of criminal activity, and may result from fear that something is going to be lost or not gained. Fear based living is often thought to be symbolic of the words *False Evidence Appearing Real,* and when a person lives in fear that is a crime against their own life or kingdom. We are reminded by the Holy Bible which is a written book that symbolizes life-- that we each are the manuscript ourselves. That is, the kingdom of heaven is at hand and since most people have two hands or the representation of such. Perhaps it would be proper to say that you can see yourself as being doubly blessed with royalty in all areas of your life. That might help to bring the concept of recovering health and creating wealth a little clearer into focus. In order to help the world become an even better place to live you have to have an awesome personal vision, because you cannot impart to others what you do not have. Quite often a person participates in all kinds of services and activities that help to accomplish phenomenal goals for other people and organizations but rarely acknowledge that their contribution is a statement of their own greatness as well. One aspect of introspection is seeing yourself as a foundation that is well established when you are helping others to excel so that you don't lose sight of who you are and be come enslaved in other people's programming of life.

I highly recommend a technique that will help you to be successful as you practice introspection and progress from fear based living consisting of what life will dole out to you as a result of following all of the precepts of others; the technique is simply stepping up to the art of defining your own concept of <u>G</u>ood

Orderly Direction or, the shortened pronouncement is GOD, which carries with it the mandatory sentence of "to thine own self be true". The majority of the organizations in society, and especially programs with a nucleus of honesty, open mindedness, and an action cue of doing the next right thing, such as Twelve Step Facilitation therapy, practice quality living based on this idea of defining **GOD,** which I state as **Good Orderly Direction.** Your life experiences from the beginning of time provide reinforcing tools that will be valuable as you practice conscious introspection to keep up with your own spiritual housekeeping to provide better service to and build healthier relationships with others. Spiritual housekeeping is the process of looking at the past momentarily to see how it can be thought about differently, and how pertinent aspects of the information can be rewritten based on how you see things today. It is part of the cognitive processing that we read about in psychology where we examine how we learn, memorize, and recall information. Sometimes we may find it difficult to redefine or even understand the importance of changing the data bank/ information recorded in our brain when there has been trauma or other adverse experiences. This challenge of temporarily not being able to learn a new way to look at your own knowledge or classify information is called interference, and is noted to be the result of old information getting in the way or popping up when you attempt to learn or assemble new data. We will discuss how to move beyond that particular obstacle throughout the book.

Remember, **FOCUS** on your own life first because this paves a way to help others remember the joy of believing in themselves. If you have ever flown on an airplane you will recall the flight attendants will usually remind you that if there is a change in cabin pressure during the flight the oxygen masks will automatically drop from the overhead compartments. They also remind you to put your oxygen mask on first and then assist children or other passengers as needed. Portions of the next statement changes the words around a bit in order to suggest that you can understand a different way of looking at pretty much any situation in life for the purpose of keeping your path clear when you walk towards your taller intellectual perspective or proper calling in life. Sometimes it may seem like a little bit of discrimination when we read or hear about the culture of the "Jew" and I recall hearing as a child: "to the Jew first and then to the Gentile". So I suggest that we read or look at that statement as: taking care of the one that is with you <u>or the word Jew spelled differently as you listen for the thought or sound following</u> (wej/widyou) which is yourself, first and then wise as serpents and the word Gentile can transform as well to become "gentle" as doves because all humans are also gods (good people with <u>o</u>rder in their lives and <u>d</u>irected by their own good wisdom).

The last statement suggests that you acknowledge yourself always, and remember when helping others that they know best what is needed for themselves. And don't be offended if a person sees things differently than you or if they apply principles in a manner other than you would in their own lives.

Gods Themselves

When I was a little girl my Aunt Cleo insured that I went to church on most Sundays. I was a junior usher and even got baptized a-g-a-i-n. You know the original baptismal pool and the male's or female's walk on water occurs when in the uterus. We float around in the chorion fully immersed in the amniotic fluid for 9 months, meditate on that.... However, that true understanding of oneness and Good Orderly Direction or who God is escaped me until I was 30 something but I've been watching and for the most part consciously growing ever since.

There are so many things jockeying for position in a person's life that the authentic plans that one writes for making this world a better place, "once I get there", when I am given up to birth or born into the earth's atmosphere become overshadowed. And in the quest to remember the primary purpose of improving one's own life to help the world be a better place to live, the sidetracking of priorities takes place and self is lost in it all.

For me, after many opportunities to grow also known as life challenges that I have overcome, which included serious dysfunctional family relationships, alcohol and other drugs and addictions, multiple bad marriages, a diagnosis of brief reactive psychosis that escalated to schizoaffective disorder (bipolar) and "time out" in the form of incarceration, I grasped a viable concept of Good Orderly Direction and I believe that the passages of this book will help you to get out of your comfort zone and onto the dance floor of life, and waltzing as a much more successful being as you come to define a one to one relationship of God (good orderly direction) and self. You might say that you are the one lord, one faith, and the one baptism of your own life. It is imperative that I note that spiritual growth and development is an awesome ever changing aspect of life. Therefore you will always need to keep your dreams/goals in the forefront of your mind and written on a tablet per the book of Habakkuk 2:2 of the Holy Bible because they are the personification of you, God.

Without a definition of good orderly direction, as you understand God, life becomes symbolic of flying a remote control model airplane with bad wires; after a while the plane just crashes and burns. This is an analogy of what can also happen in peoples' lives. They wander along on the journey of life attempting to fill a void that doesn't really exist but seems so because of all of the external activity directed towards others. Mind you now, that if introspection is coupled with dream building, lots of self forgiveness, belief in self, and self appreciation, then the scope of help to others automatically multiplies immensely. It will become second nature to integrate a portion of self into the idea of helping to make the world a better place--- especially because you exist. From this perspective, the process of reaching out is more balanced and healthy in application.

So I highly suggest that you see yourself as a ***Good*** person - with an ***Orderly*** life - ***Directed*** by the wholeness of your own spirit or energy source, yes as the ***GOD*** of your own life, with trust and faith in the decisions that you make and with great expectations for the successful and positive manifestation concerning the visions that you have regarding the greatness of your life. I have heard many times in the Twelve Step Rooms that "it was my best thinking that got me here". I would like to make an additional affirmation and say that "it is truly a fact that I am also energy known as intelligence, and that that is what got me to planet earth and I have done a very good job adjusting to it all, I might add". Another way to see the definition of God is to think about the term "desire". If you shun the word or do not see a reason to believe that you are worthy of the good and prosperous things in life like good health, material blessings, healthy relationships, and wealth that might be an indication that the time spent directing your thoughts and resources towards other peoples' goals is out of balance. However, when utilizing introspection with the understanding that you will have more to share with others as a result, you insure that your life/kingdom is in tact. When the acronym GOD is defined as Good Organized Desire then your life will symbolize good ideas that are organized to bring about the desires of your heart (or mind) for the creation of greater dreams and their manifestation in your own kingdom/life.

Let's say, for example, that you have a desire to become licensed as a physician. We know that in order to accomplish that goal you would have to complete a curriculum of math and science classes. The good aspect is recognized in the understanding that helping people who are sick is a good thing; even if you have papers and books all over the place at mid-term examination time you would still be organized because you are staying focused through the implementation of a conscious plan to reach your goal. Lastly the desire aspect was understood in the beginning. Another one of my favorite motivational speakers, Effie Reid, says that "you begin with the end in mind". In this instance it is clear that it was desire to help others be well that prompted the idea to realize the dream of becoming a physician. If this all sounds very simple then that's a good thing because it is so important to (1) believe in oneself, (2) believe that your dreams will come true, and (3) believe that your life is truly worthy to be blessed with the good and prosperous gifts that you have envisioned. This is especially so when complexities in life attempt to overshadow the basics of GOD (good orderly direction) suggesting that others can but you cannot realize your fondest dreams.

If you will recall, the chapter on **FOCUS** suggests that **A**ttitude **A**djustment is an important tool that you can use to bring about the realization of your dreams and goals. It is also considered behavior modification when you add to or take away from traditional words or definitions implementing changes to see new meaning in your own life. This technique of introspection where you become a change agent managing your own personal space for the purpose of consistently moving along the path of life towards taller intellectual understandings, will be helpful in maintaining mental stamina and supporting recovery from physical, financial, psychological or spiritual maladies.

It is written in the book of Psalm 46:10 of the Holy Bible "be still and know that "I AM God". Do you think perhaps the letter "a" is not seen or understood between the words "AM" and "God"? If you were studying to be a secretary or administrative assistant that takes dictation you might be required to learn shorthand. This procedure takes words and drastically shortens the spelling by designing the alphabet symbols as little strokes and lines of the pen. For example (,) represents the word "is", (_) represents the word "and" etc. imagine that!

The medical profession is another arena that applies a huge array of symbols in its communication process: I am sure that you remember that "bid" represents twice a day for taking medication, "tx" is symbolic for the word treatment, and "rx" is symbolic for the word prescription. The small a with a line above it (ā) is defined as "before" as in before meals, "hs" represents hour of sleep, and the list goes on. Each day there are any number of signs and symbols created to help you achieve your goals in a manner that is most logical for you. Lawyers and judges utilize one degree of understanding, physicians and nurses use another, and architects or those drilling for oil use another still. And each human being has to evolve (grow) to understand his/her own language. Conscious spiritual growth and development is basic to living a healthy well balanced life and this is best accomplished by consistent attitude adjustments with the understanding that there is always another way to look at situations in life. The mail room clerk, word processor, computer analyst, security guard, human resources personnel, supervisors, maintenance staff, department heads, and chief executive officers of various organizations all have different tasks to perform at varying times however, their purposes for working within the organization are to (1) accomplish or provide a venue of growth for accomplishing their own goals and (2) help others experience success at realizing their goals. For example, when you are employed you are helping the organization to realize their mission and you are also blessing your own life by looking at yourself and consistently applying your wisdom and talents which bring about salary increases whereby your own value is enhanced.

The process of reaching and sustaining recovery in the physical, spiritual, mental, financial, and relationship aspects of your life is very similar to the previous organizational example. Each person has billions of brain cells called gray matter. The understanding that there are so many brain cells indicates that you are free to achieve many things in your life, but more importantly, there are numerous ways in which to think about accomplishing those things. Each human being is also an organizational unit or complete system of systems themselves. We have the cardiovascular system, the musculoskeletal system, endocrine system, etcetera of our bodies and the healthy balanced processing of information via attitude adjustments so that all aspects of the whole system are working as they should to accomplish its own mission is imperative for the individual to be able to work with and help others complete their goals and realize their dreams. This concept of consistently practicing the adjustment of attitudes will instill confidence and after a while it will be second nature to see yourself as having the victory in every aspect of your life even before the occurrence of life changing situations are evident.

Another popular and often overlooked idea that is widely used throughout the world is that of ACRONYMS. They are seen and pronounced all the time, yet because you may be so well tuned to things outside of self the process of what has taken place when you see an acronym will go right over your head. They are usually capital letters that represent some idea or association. Popular acronyms are: USA, for United States of America, or USA, for United States Army; VA, for the state of Virginia, or VA, for the Veterans Affairs organization; NATO, for the National Alliance Treaty Organizations; CNO, for Chief of Naval Operations; CEO, for Chief Executive Officer; DO, for Division Officer; BMW, for the Bavarian Motor Works automobile, GMU, for George Mason University; CNU, for Christopher Newport University; and the most popular usage is from the USPS, United

States Postal Service, the abbreviations or acronyms for all of the states in the USA. I am commenting on this topic because it helps to bring to light the reason why personal goals and dreams may sometimes not even be thought about not to mention written down on a piece of paper or in a tablet. It is not unusual for a person to get caught up in someone else's idea or dream and their own becomes totally disregarded. And after a while the individual begins to think that there is a void or emptiness in his/her own life when in actuality their own spirit begins to scan the brain, if you will, to determine where the energy from its kingdom is going, similar to an inventory. I believe that when we clap for others energy or chemicals are released in the brain and when we clap for ourselves there is also an energy or chemical reaction. When the individual's spirit or energy source checks to see the results of the release of energy if it is all to another's glory, and one's own kingdom is unconsciously being glorified, the message from oneself is sent to oneself that self is being short changed. I think this is represented by a feeling of being void or lonely often times. This imbalance in energy utilization can lead to a reliance on other spirits such cigarettes, alcohol, street drugs, gross prescription drug usage, immoral sexual activity or being overly attracted by other peoples' energy (spirit), gambling, attempting to control other people, places, and circumstances because of fear of failure, and other mental illnesses or maladies. You may now be able to more clearly see the importance of regularly reminding yourself that you are a good person, with order in your life, and how being directed by your own good wisdom is paramount. In other words remembering that you are the lord of your own life or captain of your own ship. This statement about **g**ood **o**rderly **d**irection is frequently made because it is so easy to forget yourself or be misled to go chasing after someone else's dream.

Mark Gorman, a very powerful inspirational speaker, cautions people to "Act Like Your Dream"!

So to consistently realize yourself as a good person, with order in your life, being directed by your own good knowledge, or if you see yourself as having a large successful organization or business one day, or being able to go shopping anytime you want to, or freely giving to charitable causes without becoming a charity case yourself, then you must mentally prepare, apply, and conduct yourself in that manner. Dream building is an excellent way to help you accomplish this freedom of looking at yourself with approval. Dream building is window shopping with a serious belief and expectation that the dreams will come true because you will also be performing the actions for it to be so. When you avail yourself to the attitude adjustments of acknowledging yourself as being good, orderly living, and directed by your own good quality wisdom the situations in life that appear monumental are easily right sized and the wholeness of your being or the wholeness of your own spirit is able to maintain the atmospheric quality required for the manifestation and realization of your dreams as you also help others to excel without getting lost in their space or circumstances.

The idea of introspection resulting from continuous attitude adjustments may sound selfish because we are taught to reach out to others or to pray for others but the other part of that statement: "in order that you may be made well" is sometimes forgotten; need to read that again? Pray for others so that you may be made well or so that you will stay well and balanced (Holy Bible, James 5:16). Therefore, all your words are basically prayers for yourself. That takes you to the earlier pages of this book to remember that you exist to help the world to be a better place by being the best person that you can be. A very successful business owner and another of my favorite speakers by the name of Lennon Ledbetter suggests that you "build a better you" and I believe the more you appreciate yourself the more other people are helped by your example of kindness to yourself. Therefore, when you are focused on your dreams and goals it is easier to allow others to grow and become their best without feeling that you have failed if the outcome of plans concerning them are different from your ideas about how things could be. I have been reminded many times by my friend, Linda, that "expectations concerning others may be resentments waiting to happen". So when my energy is equally divided to attend to my kingdom first which displays an example for others to emulate, if they wish, then the relationships have room for growth and society will be blessed because of the harmony in my life.

I would like to share at this point that you are always, sometimes unconsciously and other times with awareness, drawing a spiritual picture of yourself and since we are all gods (good people, with order in our lives, directed by our own good knowledge) we have wisdom and insight and there is also that continuous subconscious or unconscious reading of information generated by others. Being spiritual beings and composed of the power of protons, neutrons, and electrons it just makes sense to understand that registering the energy of other beings or humans is second nature. In order to develop a system of looking at your kingdom or body and viewing the bones or organs, a process called x-ray, man would have to be the constituent of x-ray him/her self, don't you think? That's another one of those situations where you cannot give something that you do not have. In order to create technology we recognize that we are technology ourselves.

I believe the accomplishments of one's goals and dreams is basically dependent upon how and which talents they choose to hone and there certainly are numerous choices of ideas to explore for reaching taller grounds of successful living since each person has literally hundreds of thousands of pathways by which to apply their knowledge.

When I speak of a spiritual life I am also reminded of the sayings that we hear during hurricane season or during thunderstorms: "an act of God". Frequently we see the term as something other than oneself that is distant or untouchable. However, if you recall that while we do not see the wind blow, most of the time, we can see the leaves on the trees moving when the god or element called wind is at work. Sometimes you may be propelled along the street and have to button your coat in the winter because of the actions of the spirit/god called wind but its composition remains invisible. So we do not see the wind we see the results of the actions of the wind and this is similar to the human life. You are the artist drawing the pictures and so with childlike faith you want to develop beautiful, life producing, happy and colorful scenes in order that others will see the level of positive reception and knowledge that you have concerning yourself. Without the true spiritual work that is experienced in introspection, your life might always be depicted in the light of mental illnesses such as depression, loss of concentration and memory or other spiritual maladies known as psychopathies that appear as robbery, murder, addictions, rape, financial chaos, recidivism, or the unseparable belief in little white lies. By the way, one of those lies is that Corporate America is white or that there is a group of people actually the color of white. There really are no people of white color in our society. The culture of people called Caucasian are actually pinkish and if you hold a piece of typing paper up to their face or by their arm it becomes evident that all people are colored; however, none are white. Hence, the little white lie. Another one of those lies is that all brown skinned people are from Africa or are to be called black or African Americans. I was born in Murfreesboro, NC, and my complexion is brown in color so I have adjusted to checking the box called "other" when it comes to demographics. In actuality it is the so called little things that can, if they are other than true, bring about a tremendous stronghold on your spiritual growth and development which can hamper your understanding of higher order intelligence, or belief that your ever increasing knowledge of GOD is more than sufficient to live your own life, causing you to lie and say that you don't have the knowledge that others have or just keep you in the financial sludge pool of mediocrity; therefore it is important to commit to memory the adage: "to thine own self be true".

When an individual practices the acceptance of applying whatever someone else says without allowing his/her own spirit to process the information for the reason of considering what it means to self, an access route for pathological lying and eventual lack of faith in self and others develops. The need to broaden perspectives may also go unrealized which can result in extremely dysfunctional relationships, consistently negative attitudes that sound like " I can't get anything done", "I never have my way", "why do I need to change", "I don't believe what happened", "that's a new idea, they can't do that because we've always done things this way", etc. etc. etc. In other words there will be a very high <u>r</u>esistance <u>t</u>o <u>c</u>hange (RTC) factor. The consequences of this kind of attitude are many unfulfilled dreams, intense levels of negative stress, envy, inability to make good quality decisions although the experiences in life reflect a different picture, lack of confidence in self, a super inferiority complex, fear of people and failure, and the list goes on. The practice of introspection and recognizing that all people are the god (good orderly direction) of themselves will help prevent the sluggish mental aura where the above listed conditions can thrive.

Issues

On the next few pages we will look at some of the things in life that can distract you from dream building, introspection, goal planning, and remembering that you are a good person with great order in your life directed by your own good wisdom. When the negative characteristics of the following issues are prevalent your ability to effectively help other people excel is hindered.

Learned Attitudes

I am sure that you have heard the saying "children learn what they live". It is also written that we are fashioned in the likeness of God. Some versions of the Holy Bible write "In the image of God created he them". Let's look at the word *He* for a second. The letter *H resembles a goalpost on the football field, don't you agree? We know that each human is also a spiritual being and with childlike faith it is easier to see the word He* as meaning the goal of the individual's spirit was to create a vessel for its own dwelling and your existence in the human form is proof of that. When we look at the acronyms or shorthand versions in life again, the letter *e* could be symbolic of the word Emmanuel which can be spelled with the letter "E" or "I" and is defined as "god is with us". We recall too that each kingdom or human being is also the trinity which is defined as the Godhead or god the father, god the sun, and god the wholeness of the individual's spirit, all three equal one. So now you can also state that the knowledge of God is in the cranium of each person, female as well as male and remove some of the discriminatory attitudes that may crop up when we see the word "He" which is used almost exclusively in our society in the reference to God. This is a prejudice that can severely hamper spiritual growth and development but I am certain that **JTB** will help you to set your sights so that your kingdom is glorified. It is also important to recognize that it is the individual's own spirit that has chosen to create him or her as a male or female as they were born. The birth of a child has very little to do with the body fluids or flesh of the servants/parents. Although the servants/parents truly have an exceptionally important job because they are trusted to help the infant to grow and to remember what she or he said they were going to do or become in order to help the world to be an even greater place to live. A little more food for thought as you practice the art of heightening your esteem via self approval.

Now, getting back to the statement of being created in the image of God. When I think about that statement I am reminded that if I walk outside when the sun is shining or even indoors in certain lights I can see my own shadow which is another word for image or likeness, so would you not agree that you are created in your own image and that it is appropriate to call yourself a, GOD, good person with order in your life directed by your own good wisdom? Another one of those points to ponder. By now the definition of good orderly direction should not be such an "ah ha" statement but one that sounds natural to your ears and that assists with the realignment of your focus when you get sidetracked. You should also be checking to see how you are acknowledging the concept of good orderly direction in all situations. It is most appropriate to be reflective and to assess the composition of your own life since the very fibers of your being make little or no sense to another. But more importantly, if it appears that a person or society has no clue as to how great you are, do not be dismayed. If you were to begin to describe who you are from the highest heights a natural phenomena that would take place would be: the person or people listening would automatically begin to scan their data banks for their own identification. That is introspection from the unconscious level and it may be the reason why you may have to read pages in a book over again or you miss information when sitting in a meeting or even while talking with others . The great author, Dale Carnegie, has written "that people really want to talk to you about themselves". I believe this is because you are important, and you know it, even if you don't always show it. Consequently, in the process of experiencing your existence and as another one of my favorite speakers, Dexter Yeager, says you will sometimes "take a few steps forward and one step back" while climbing to taller levels of success so I believe it is important to be disciplined and pay attention to the still small voice of your own understanding whilst walking through life in order to regard the information that is most important and govern yourself in the most appropriate manner to be able to help others excel as you establish the example of good orderly direction.

The statement, "this you do in remembrance of me" may be familiar to you. At first glance it seems that someone is telling you to bear in mind something regarding someone other than yourself. And, I really believe that the wholeness of your spirit, and remember each person does have his or her own spirit not one individual is alone, is basically advising, you the kingdom, that it has created, to be aware that all of the actions that you take are to be based on the knowledge and the understanding of your experiences in life and to keep in mind, the way in which your spirit, also understood as the who.le or holy spirit, has processed the information stored in your cranium. Therefore the consciousness of who "I AM" or actually who you are is well worth noting at all times. Looking at the language arena and as was stated earlier we each have a language or understanding that is peculiar to ourselves so English as a second language has very little to do with persons born outside of the United States. It is relevant to us all. My youngest daughter, Carla

Ginyne (that's her first and middle name) often says good bye to me when we are ending our telephone conversations by stating "love you longtime". I translate that to mean that she has had the knowledge that she is a God, a good person with order in her life, and directed by her own good wisdom, since the beginning of time. We will look at the word "love" again in later pages.

The book of I Corinthians 11:28 of the Holy Bible advocates to "let a man examine himself". As you apply the "Just the Basics" principles it will probably become apparent to you that you are composed of positive energy which can be symbolic of **g**oodness. There's another "g" word. Moreover, the arrangement of your energy is methodical in that the DNA chain is representative of sequence but only your hairdresser, the whole spirit of your kingdom truly knows what it is. Even with all the technology that we have available to us there are still some very good things that only the wholeness of your spirit can reveal. In particular, that you are on a path or journey in life moving towards a taller intellectual mission; performing a symphony, if you will, called your understanding of life with your own spirit (energy) directing the orchestra. Your purpose being to glorify the kingdom of heaven and since the "kingdom of heaven is at hand" according to the Holy Bible in the book of Matthew 3:2 and you have two hands or the representation of such seen as a double portion (2 hands) then surely you have to become the best person you can be with all the trimmings.

This coming of age or taking the time to allow your spirit to reveal the plan of your life to you may be manifested through the goals of completing a college degree, acquiring material blessings such real estate, an automobile, becoming debt free, changing careers, and having the time to enjoy the fruits of your labor in healthy relationships with family and acquaintances during and after becoming wealthy.

These things all represent various facets of spiritual growth and development and there would be a serious imbalance in your life if you were to be consistently introspective, applying the wisdom of God, yourself, in all situations to keep your spiritual housekeeping up to par and then be materially, financially, and physically bankrupt all the time. If you will recall at the beginning of this topic, we spoke about the learning of children. This early education may be used very well as coping strategies during the most impressive years of development. However, in order for you to remember the schemas which are a set of directions or patterns stored in your gray matter, and there is a schema for everything you do, you will have to change the old definitions by adding to or subtracting from what you have learned in your childhood years. Then the wisdom you impart to others will reflect your current perception of life. This is what will take you to your own level of greatness moving from survival to earned abundance and prosperity from your own kingdom. Keep in mind that the unfolding of new definitions in life is pretty much the only constant there is.

We have actually been practicing that principle in the pages of this book by applying different and I believe healthy classifications to old words and thoughts in a manner that will assist in the destruction of the strongholds of fear that can blind and keep you from seeing how blessed you are and what a blessing your existence is to others. For example, using the acronym GOD (good person, orderly life, directed by your own wisdom) to describe, you the person, rather than suggesting that the understanding of the word should be reserved for a day of death when someone is going to either cremate you or embalm you with formaldehyde. And then pretending that you will see someone sitting in a huge chair judging you as you walk along streets way beyond the clouds where airplanes or space ships have not yet reached; but you have to be careful because if you don't punch the right ticket while you are alive then you may not have the right of passage to that unreachable place called heaven according to that story.

I tell you the truth, your are born of your own spirit which is a word for intelligence or energy that has evolved as a result of proper conditions and that equates to: you are a spiritual being that has become a human being and I adjure you to bear in mind that life is a symbolic experience therefore your brain is figurative of the clouds or heavens and the rest of your body is the fertile land of growth and miracles itself representing the good earth. Keep in mind also that the male body is symbolic of goodness and grace as is the female's; and it is the wisdom or the result of the processing of information by the individual's spirit that is worshipped rather than the flesh. We praise the results of the functioning of each person's energy source or spirit. It is what you do not visibly see but have the faith and understanding at the subconscious and for those who practice introspection, also conscious levels, concerning your own kingdom that truly exemplifies your own super natural power.

That is probably where the statement I can do all kinds of great things because I am wonderfully made, comes from. From infancy to the fullness of dispensation also known as quality maturity the human being is constantly growing , developing, and changing. So enjoy the journey and learn to appreciate the importance of attitudinal adjustments. Your ability to excel in every area of your life depends on it!

Adversities in Life

A practice that can produce an internal conflict resulting in misfortune and seriously lowering your self esteem is that of participating in activities when you really believe in something other than what you are doing. The Quixtar business model describes it as "wanting to be somewhere else, doing something else, for yourself". When you rely on the knowledge of others and overlook the wisdom of God (your own good orderly living directed by the goodness of your own spirit) you will most likely get pretty comfortable being a follower. If that is the case, the growth from the work of your true abilities to have your light or spirit shine and to help make a positive difference in the world may be stunted. There might also be the low self esteem habit of settling for whatever someone else thinks is best for you along with the   attitude of a "poverty thinking" way of life. When any attempt is made to modify that way of living after it has been indulged in for a while, major malfunctions in the comfort zone of mediocrity that you will have found so easy to adapt to will occur because someone else would have been performing the mental calisthenics, or practicing the principles that you have been reading about in this book. It is a requirement to process information leading to "right thinking" for your own life which leads to true happiness and peace even in the midst of storms. The concept of being a leader has more to do with walking along the path of life beside others because you are led by your own good wisdom and you understand where you are going and how you are going to get there more so than having someone give you control of their life or follow you.

You want your life to embody more than the Batman and Robin television series where you are just going along and each venture that someone else dictates becomes the ride of your life simply because someone else says so. The true meaning and appreciation for your own existence is often overlooked in those instances.

One sure way to discover that your arms are too short to box with yourself, God, is to consistently expect others to pretend to lead you rather than understanding that when you pace yourself it is easier to see the intelligence revealed by your own spirit and that is what will lead you best. This small adjustment of your attitude, via checking to see that you are guided by your own wisdom throughout the day, when practiced without fail, will also be the guiding source to help you begin to recognize when to make other amendments in your decision making processes. Therefore, if you get out there and blaze new trails others will see how they too can make a difference not only in their own lives but also in the world because of the uniqueness of their kingdom. We are all gods (**g**ood people with **o**rder in our lives and **d**irected by our own good wisdom) and at the same time we are all wonderfully different. I believe that the idea of sharing your wisdom and your life experiences with others are major components in accomplishing lasting success. Reaching out to others and reminding them that they too are gods (good people with order in their lives and directed by their own good wisdom) is vital in healthy spiritual growth and development. Healthy is a key word here because it has been said by the pulpit's finest that "God will bless you in your mess"; however, that in and of itself is not necessarily a healthy thing. And if you will note, the tone of the last sentence kind of shifts your direction to someone or some other entity doing the blessing when it needs to be understood that it is always your own spirit or energy source that sends the message out and about resulting in the myriad prosperity received in life. By the way, it is well to note that I can capitalize the "G" in the word god as it pertains to myself but you will have to grow and according to another one of my favorite motivational speakers, Scott Michael says, and "raise the opinion that you have of yourself". When you have accomplished the necessary growth I believe that you will then tell the world that you are a capital GOD!

In order to recover from the adversities that are experienced when you turn your will and life over to the care of others, your belief system has to be reinforced with the understanding that whatever has transpired in life, you are still a **g**ood person with an **o**rganized life, and free to be **d**irected by your own good wisdom.

The recollection of these gems coupled with a huge dream and the willingness but more than being willing is necessary, you must take the action to promptly right wrongs or misunderstandings in order to reap the phenomenal rewards and increased number of achieved goals not to mention the personal satisfaction and serenity of seeing yourself as being victorious in all aspects of your life at all times. Something else that is required to consistently recollect who you are is self forgiveness which is our next topic.

<u>Self Forgiveness</u>

The music of self forgiveness sounds like this: I am a good person, I have order in my life, and I am directed by my own good wisdom. I forgive myself for acts of omission or commission that transpired yesterday, those that might happen today, and the things that could develop tomorrow. I am a capital GOD! I am an exceptionally good person, living life with order and tranquility, because I realize that my own spirit is what has created, leads and guides me. I appreciate all things about myself and if there is something that I need to change in order to be a better person, then I will.

One of the major elements used to destroy relationships and nations is that of holding grudges. However, I have found that if I am harmed by someone or some organization or thing it is always best for me to look into my toy box of life and find something to forgive myself for. Then my negative energy is changed to a positive light and the entity bringing the harm has one less source of influence to block the life of its own spirit and they are apt to create a way to amend the wrong or tort in a way that brings about a greater amount of good for a greater number of people. No doubt before the opportunity to harm me was revealed, there were probably many others along the path of life who were despitefully used or abused.

When I look at the harm that I may have caused others, it is extremely important that I make things right and balanced by (1) forgiving myself and recognizing that my actions will be seen as a "sign" of applying my talents in a way that did not consider the capital "G", so the word "sign" when the understanding that I am a God or "G" is removed, becomes the word "sin" which now has a negative connotation. So you see it is important to remember who you are in every situation. Sometimes in life you will have to adjust the historical monumental ideas of even the giants of the past such as Einstein whose law of relativity says that "for every action there is an equal and opposite reaction". The **JTB** concept suggests that "when the situation is positive, make it even more positive and when the situation is other than positive, make it positive"! This practice becomes easy to accomplish when you are consistently learning to see more ways in which your actions reflect that you are a great person with order in your life being directed by your own good information.

Post Traumatic
Stress Disorder

An extremely traumatic event that you experience which results in the feelings of helplessness, intense fear or dreadfulness or that renders you like a needle stuck in the groove of a record repeatedly talking about the incident and associating most things in life to the negative event, rather than recognizing how good orderly direction transformed the event into something positive, is considered **Post Traumatic Stress Disorder**. This malady can steal your dreams, cause you to forget to establish goals and simply settle for the bare minimum in life and abandoning your prosperity even though the outward appearances suggest that you have it all together. Things might be going well, at least you think so, that is , until there is a change in life's daily circumstances. For instance, the sun shines instead of rain like the local weather channel announced or a problem arises and another person-- it could be your physician, the minister, your spouse, or an associate talks to you about a solution or a pathway to a solution for the challenge and instead of looking at viable options and processing information to clear the drawing board (another word for your mind) for the inscription of new definitions concerning it all and get moving ahead with life, you repeatedly talk about the very stressful event while denying or not even registering that anything at all could ever help in the situation. The event can subtly or very overtly shadow the positive aspects of your life. It can literally put healthy purposeful living on hold while you unconsciously walk around in the maze of yesteryear. Unfortunately PTSD doesn't click right in so that the symptoms are easily recognized unless you have a history of experience in the active war zone with the military then it would be general practice to note. Spouse abuse, other physical or sexual violence including rape, being in a serious accident, or emotional abuse can also result in PTSD.

Perhaps it could be the internal protection mode that we all have which allows the individual to sometimes live in a seemingly healthy fashion, albeit not at the tallest levels of quality, for long periods of time beyond the traumatic event without diagnosis. PTSD may be coupled with or masked by other disorders such as anxiety, depression or obsessive compulsive disorders. The key to moving ahead after something that seriously impacts your life in that manner is to be courageous and report it to a friend, police officer, physician or someone who can help you get to the appropriate facilities and receive the therapeutic psychological help that you need. Group therapy is a good way to look at the incident and determine what aspects to work on regarding the attitudinal changes required to get back onto the playing field for your own life and out of the little box that times like those can create for you to crawl into. Practicing the mental calisthenics of seeing how many good things you can note about yourself and writing them on a piece of paper as well as verbally reminding yourself that you are also a god: that is, a person with **g**reat self appreciation, **o**rdered by the understanding of the completeness of your own being, and **d**irected by your own spirit towards even greater successes in your own life which will help others to excel regardless of the former negative experiences. Knowing that "this too shall pass" will help you to have positive expectations for future happenings in your own life.

The last few sentences were written with the word "own" appearing frequently because when your life has been violated it is important to regain possession by positive affirmations that result in positive actions that realign your focus towards your goals. You will also be able to gather meekness and strength to recognize and move beyond other occurrences that could possibly transpire.

The majority of the time the inability to change old tapes and harmful situations recorded in your brain, into bridges that are paths to healthy qualitative living, is the result of anger, pain, shame, guilt, lust, envy, or confusion originating either from the person harmed or by the person bringing the harm. A good attitude along with the appropriate medical care will help you to live for the purpose of living life abundantly, one step at a time, one day at a time, dreaming greater dreams as you overcome the hurdles associated with PTSD.

Alcohol, Illegal And Prescription Drug Addictions, And Other <u>Mental Illnesses</u>

According to Alcoholics (AA) and Narcotics Anonymous (NA) the diseases associated with these fellowships are manifested by a mental obsession or craving and a physical allergy. ALANON is the recovery support group structured for the family and friends affected by the challenges of those with the mental illness of substance abuse. I would like to note that if you are a person with a mental illness of alcoholism or other drug abuse then you should learn to become your own best friend. For that reason, taking the time to listen to your spirit from the ALANON rooms may also be a good therapy for you.

Now looking at the first paragraph again, the allergy part is symbolic in that when the substances are utilized the results are often adverse and the individual does not know when or what will take place when they are under the influence of a spirit other than their own. However, like the person who is allergic to a bumble bee sting or an injection of penicillin, the individual suffering with these illnesses does know that the results can be a fatal situation either immediately or in time when the substance infiltrates their system. There could be an accident, death, a fight, convulsions, or inappropriate spending of money or giving one's valuables to others in situations that do not necessarily warrant an action of that nature.

The ingestion of alcohol, illegal drugs, or the abuse of prescription drugs or sexual immorality are not the sole reasons for mental illness. Sometimes the brain chemicals become imbalanced, I believe, due to improper thinking and inattention to the care given to oneself which may, in some instances, lead to the addictions . You have been reading about some of those things that can short change your kingdom and rob you of your dreams leaving you with low self respect and minimal desire to make efforts toward goal establishments or completions.

The Merriam-Webster dictionary terms one characterization of the word spirit as being a distilled alcoholic liquor and in other dictionaries it is listed as an element that can overcome or change a situation. Many years ago the bottles of alcoholic beverages also had the word "spirits" printed on them. When your dreams are left to the enhancement of spirits other than your own (remember you have a who.le or you are the holy spirit yourself) they get lost in the altered state because the situation of other things commanding your life is unnatural. You may have noticed that **JTB** is a very redundant manuscript and that is because in order to become perfect and it is written that you are perfect according to how you use the knowledge in your cranium. That means that the data from your brain will be perfect for you to utilize and accomplish your goals. However, if in the course of a conversation someone that you are speaking with chooses to apply a principle that you have used to create a positive situation in your life, then that individual will have to change the information to express the understanding for him or her self and then apply the principle.

You may both make the statement: " I washed my hair and it to grew to be long and healthy ". And you might be using SATINIQUE hair care products and the other person may have chosen to use L'OREAL however the bottom line is that you both utilized the wisdom from your own craniums/brain cells to accomplish the goal of good hair care and growth, which is perfection, excellence, or precision, you choose the word. I think that you will agree that redundancy can be a good thing which leads to the connection of other information revealing myriad ways to see and appreciate life.

For example in order for the toddler to become proficient at balance, parents will often invest in a walker very early in life so they can scoot around the house, get exercise and be around the other family members while becoming more independent at the same time. Then as time goes on the trusted servants purchase a tricycle which has three wheels. The toddler practices and practices and practices which is another way to show redundancy and soon there is the purchase of a bicycle which has two wheels and training wheels on the rear of the vehicle and because the child is self determined and has mastered the art of being redundant for good purposes, the time soon arrives when the training wheels are removed from the bicycle and the results of the child's study of equilibrium, gravity, etcetera is demonstrated as they pronounce "look mom or dad I can ride my bicycle with no hands".

Another very vital exercise in redundancy is that of breathing. We perform it unconsciously and as was written earlier **JTB** is designed to help you become more conscious of the magnificent human being that you are. This will help you remember that you have all knowledge, which is another word for power, to accomplish your greatest dreams and goals. By the way if you disagree with the relationship between breathing and redundancy, scroll through your data banks and key in on the time when you were growing and developing in the uterus. Oxygen and all of the components were present in the amniotic fluid however you did not need to physically use the lungs to breathe. The active process of breathing began once you were in the earth's atmosphere. The point here is redundancy is exemplified by the transformation from passive to active breathing.

Along with those principles, if you purpose to modify the word GOD and expand it to read as **g**ood **o**rderly **d**irection which we have been doing all through the book, you will have performed a degree of mental calisthenics that can help to make the required changes in your life easy and acceptable. I believe that if change is brought about by extreme ancillary means with the purpose being to do something other than have the world see the glory of your good orderly direction then an internal conflict ensues and the path of your life becomes detoured leading to a very timely catastrophe. Here the statement "all in God's time" presents a picture that is much more clearly seen in sobriety. That simply means that a person will arrive at whatever station he or she is headed for whenever they accomplish the work required to get there. Overindulgences or usage of substances such as nicotine, excessive caffeine, alcohol, illegal drugs, abuse of prescription drugs or other people' spirits, or receiving too much wisdom from others without taking the time to perform the mental calisthenics or to observe how the wholeness of your spirit is changing and processing the information for utilization by thy own hand, can put your dreams in cement and seemingly cast them to the bottom of the ocean.

Twelve Step Facilitation Therapy is a very effective means of restoring mental balance and achieving sobriety from the aforementioned substances which basically means living without requirements for mood altering substances. The twelve step model, to a degree, actually uses a form of the psychology technique called maintenance rehearsal which is depicted as repeating words over and over in order to help with memory, recall, and learning. However, that process can branch out into what is called elaborative rehearsal which admonishes the individual to make a connection of the new material with something familiar in order to broaden the learning curve. Each time a person attends an AA, NA, or ALANON meeting the opening reading and an explanation of how the principles work are read verbatim.

Since these principles are always the same it is called maintenance rehearsal. However, these organizations reminds those attending to associate rather than affiliate the principles when outside of the twelve step meeting rooms. That means that when applying the guidelines in daily interactions the person has to change the information or definition of the steps so that his/her experiences are redefined and presented from an even more positive perspective to help others to also excel which assists the individual to continue on their proper path in life. The principles remain the same and it is important for the application to be diverse. You could say that they have exposure to the AA, NA, or ALANON worlds but they are not of those worlds because they have transformed the information of the AA, NA, or ALANON programs in their mind. I believe the concept is designed to help those in regular attendance to also recover from the stigmas of forgetfulness and confusion that can be associated with the diseases. Thereby producing new patterns in the brain which after a while instead of being dry which is merely being without a drink or other mood altering spirits, clarity takes place and happiness, and the freedom to live a productive life without the substance abuse crutch is ubiquitous or ever present. Those processes of maintenance and elaborative rehearsal take place when you practice the JTB concept of looking at yourself and your experiences, adjusting your attitude and keeping in the forefront of your mind the fact that you are a **g**ood person with **o**rder in your life, a spiritual being that has become a human being and **d**irected by your own good wisdom. **JTB** principles are the mental exercise required to stay spiritually alert in order to realize your dreams and goals and to proclaim the victory regarding all aspects of your life especially in the arena of mental wellness experienced by breaking the chains of substance abuse and other addictions.

Need for a Greater Faith

When an individual has a lack of applied conscious faith there will be an automatic internal conflict leading to a grossly external focus which acts as a conduit for confusion. The 11th chapter of the book of Hebrews in the Holy Bible states that "faith is the assurance of things hoped for, the conviction of things not seen". This suggests that prior to the manifestation of things in life there has to be an expectation of them. **JTB** is designed to help you believe that behavior modification via the conscious processing of information and networking of the same will be of assistance in creating new definitions for your old ways of thinking. You can expect a new life filled with your own great dreams and achievements that lead to building bridges that help others to cross over into taller levels of transmutation of energy as well. Those last few words mean that you will be helping others change the way in which they are using their authority and talents for the purpose of seeing, hearing, and understanding a greater quality of intelligence.

Chapter 12 of the first book of Corinthians in the Holy Bible speaks of "the excellence of love". Keeping in mind that ye are gods, I would like to have you perform another exercise with words. But before you begin it is highly suggested that you remember that the word GOD does not change, it is always written or thought of as GOD because the human being or homo sapien kingdom is always **g**ood, designed with **o**rder, and **d**irected by its own spirit . Even when the person has performed the vilest of acts there is still some good that can be utilized from his or her own life to bring about mental stability, self forgiveness, and a better way of living if he or she is willing to change. No matter where they are located-- at home, in jail, school, on vacation, where ever! There is still an element of good that can prevail in their life.

This time you are going to take the word "love" and spell it backwards. The result is the word "evol". When you begin the process of sounding it out it travels to the word evolve; another one of those shorthand things. Again when walking according to your own spirit you will often have to mentally add to or take away from words or phrases in order to maintain psychological balance. This new word "evol" or evolve is defined as growth, development, or progress and in order to evolve or change, intelligence or knowledge is required. So the word love, when we read it inside out or upside down with childlike faith, is now a word meaning wisdom or intelligence. You have actually networked from your own experience and arrived at a different characteristic for the word love in order to make a little more sense out of everyday language. We often think of the flesh or the idea of the flesh develops shortly after speaking the word love if you have not practiced being a change agent or being introspective. I think it good to say that chapter 13 of the book of 1 Corinthians of the Holy Bible is really talking about "the excellence of wisdom" and now it may be easier to understand why one would appear to be noisy and empty if their speaking was "with the tongues of men and of angels but having no" wisdom beyond the obvious or outside of someone else's definition. Especially when it is written that 'all have been given a measure of faith". The book of Luke 24:45 in the Holy Bible says essentially that God, and it is now remembered that God is a shortened version of the words good orderly direction, opens or broadens the mind to understand the things of life. Remember too with an honest understanding that you are a good person and truly believe that your are ordered or designed in the manner that you are because you are you and that that is good. When you truthfully accept that your own authority known as your spirit directs your life when your avail yourself wholly to the things of thine own hands, then there is no topic too big or too small to be understood and positively applied to the greatness of your life at some point in time. The word scripture, I believe, means the things that are written in the spiritual first, then the mental processing takes place, and finally the physical or pen and ink elements of life evolve. And when you believe in yourself as the good order and direction of your own life, the meaning of the scriptures or things that are written pertaining to life will be constantly revealed to you. The idea of leaning towards your own knowledge as you are exposed to myriad concepts in life will help you retain focus or easily regain posture as the natural inclination to reach out to others and help them to realize their goals and dreams is practiced.

I trust that you will continue to practice the JTB principles of honesty and self efficacy also known as belief in yourself and that you will carry out the mental calisthenics regimen on a consistent basis so as to bring about a difference in your life by daring to change the way in which you process information via think, think, thinking more highly of yourself. I believe you will see and remember more clearly the plans that you have or can have for success in your life. I also believe that you will begin to see that the best way to become triumphant in the realization of your dreams is to help others accomplish their goals. The better your think of yourself the easier it is to help others without losing sight of your dreams.

When you share with others how the **JTB** principles work for you as far as moving mountains and clearing your passageway to see and understand your own rationale for dreaming greater dreams, others will also recognize how the importance of having a great vision and making similar changes in their thought processes can also work to the good for them. The idea of the **need for a greater faith** will not seem foreign; instead it will become a welcome addition to the betterment of individual lives.

The Conclusion of it All

Just the Basics is concerned greatly with the spiritual consciousness (awareness of the spiritual realm) of the individual. As was stated in the introduction my goal is to make a very positive impact in society and help all people reading this book to see themselves more clearly as the optimistic, progressive thinking, and successful winners that they are.

Humans are amazing in that we frequently walk through life accomplishing all kinds of magnificence in a state of oblivion as far as our own spiritual make up is concerned. Self appreciation as you have read is more fully realized when the wholeness of your spirit is acknowledged. Apply the principles according to "Just the Basics by Emolyne" consistently in your life, in everyday situations, in season and out of season, being thankful that you are a God, or **g**ood person with **o**rder in your life **d**irected by the wisdom imparted from your own energy source, in the remembrance of all things and I promise you that life will develop new and more authoritative personal meaning. I liken the process of spiritual growth and development to going to your favorite restaurant with all of the delicious foods that you like to eat each day of the week. It is good! And with the great food there is the requirement to exercise to burn the calories in order for the body to get the best effects from the nourishment.

While studying and applying these principles be certain to go into the world for the purpose of sharing your wisdom while also deciphering the words of all the nations or peoples. Remember you can't keep your wisdom without giving it away, how else would it come back to you? Hence, truly enjoy the banquet of life and the development of healthier relationships in view of the fact that you are an exceptionally good person with order in your life directed by your own good wisdom.

May the tranquility that surpasses the cares of the world always result from your own grace, omnipotence, and dialogue and be recognized as "Just the Basics" for you!.

<u>Notes</u>

<u>Notes</u>

<u>Notes</u>

Notes

www.ingramcontent.com/pod-product-compliance
Lightning Source LLC
Chambersburg PA
CBHW031256280526
45784CB00004B/1872